50 Cocktail and Bites Recipes

By: Kelly Johnson

Table of Contents

- Classic Martini & Parmesan Truffle Fries
- Margarita & Spicy Shrimp Tacos
- Negroni & Prosciutto-Wrapped Melon
- Old Fashioned & Smoked Almonds
- Mojito & Cuban Chicken Skewers
- Espresso Martini & Chocolate-Dipped Biscotti
- Manhattan & Mini Beef Sliders
- French 75 & Goat Cheese Crostini
- Moscow Mule & Honey Sriracha Wings
- Daiquiri & Coconut Shrimp
- Whiskey Sour & Candied Bacon
- Aperol Spritz & Caprese Skewers
- Paloma & Chili Lime Popcorn
- Piña Colada & Grilled Pineapple Bites
- Sidecar & Brie-Stuffed Figs
- Bloody Mary & Mini Lobster Rolls
- Cosmopolitan & Smoked Salmon Canapés
- Gin & Tonic & Cucumber Avocado Toast
- Rum Punch & Jamaican Jerk Chicken Bites
- Sazerac & Cajun Spiced Pecans
- Pisco Sour & Peruvian Ceviche Cups
- Amaretto Sour & Almond-Crusted Brie Bites
- Bellini & Peach Prosciutto Wraps
- Caipirinha & Brazilian Cheese Puffs
- Hot Toddy & Maple Glazed Nuts
- Kir Royale & Raspberry Dark Chocolate Tartlets
- Dark & Stormy & Spicy Ginger Meatballs
- Mai Tai & Crispy Coconut Chicken Bites
- Tom Collins & Lemon Basil Bruschetta
- Irish Coffee & Whiskey Caramel Truffles
- Blue Lagoon & Shrimp Ceviche Shots
- Hurricane & New Orleans Beignets
- Champagne Cocktail & Smoked Gouda Puffs
- Mint Julep & Bourbon Glazed Wings
- White Russian & Espresso Brownie Bites

- Black Velvet & Oysters on the Half Shell
- Gimlet & Avocado Deviled Eggs
- Zombie Cocktail & Hawaiian BBQ Skewers
- Brandy Alexander & Hazelnut Shortbread
- Clover Club & Raspberry Macarons
- Aviation & Lavender Honey Toast Points
- Tequila Sunrise & Mango Habanero Salsa
- Vesper Martini & Truffle Mushroom Arancini
- Planter's Punch & Jerk-Spiced Plantain Chips
- Spritz Veneziano & Olive Tapenade Crostini
- Mezcal Margarita & Grilled Elote Bites
- Boulevardier & Gorgonzola-Stuffed Dates
- Hanky Panky & Spicy Chorizo Empanadas
- Jungle Bird & Crispy Duck Spring Rolls
- Bee's Knees & Honey Glazed Pistachios

Classic Martini & Parmesan Truffle Fries

Classic Martini

Ingredients:

- 60ml gin
- 10ml dry vermouth
- Ice
- Lemon twist or olive, for garnish

Instructions:

1. Fill a mixing glass with ice, add gin and vermouth.
2. Stir until well-chilled, then strain into a chilled martini glass.
3. Garnish with a lemon twist or an olive.

Parmesan Truffle Fries

Ingredients:

- 500g fries
- 2 tbsp truffle oil
- 50g Parmesan, grated
- Salt and pepper
- 1 tbsp chopped parsley

Instructions:

1. Bake or fry fries until golden.
2. Toss with truffle oil, Parmesan, salt, and parsley.

Margarita & Spicy Shrimp Tacos

Margarita

Ingredients:

- 50ml tequila
- 25ml lime juice
- 15ml triple sec
- Ice
- Salt for rim
- Lime wedge

Instructions:

1. Rim glass with salt.
2. Shake tequila, lime juice, and triple sec with ice.
3. Strain into glass with fresh ice.

Spicy Shrimp Tacos

Ingredients:

- 200g shrimp, peeled
- 1 tsp chili powder
- 1 tbsp lime juice
- 1 tbsp olive oil
- 4 small tortillas
- 50g shredded cabbage
- Salsa, for topping

Instructions:

1. Toss shrimp with chili powder, lime juice, and oil.
2. Sauté until cooked.
3. Serve in tortillas with cabbage and salsa.

Negroni & Prosciutto-Wrapped Melon

Negroni

Ingredients:

- 30ml gin
- 30ml Campari
- 30ml sweet vermouth
- Ice
- Orange peel

Instructions:

1. Stir all ingredients with ice and strain into a glass.
2. Garnish with an orange peel.

Prosciutto-Wrapped Melon

Ingredients:

- 1 small cantaloupe, sliced
- 10 slices prosciutto
- 1 tbsp balsamic glaze

Instructions:

1. Wrap prosciutto around melon slices.
2. Drizzle with balsamic glaze.

Old Fashioned & Smoked Almonds

Old Fashioned

Ingredients:

- 60ml bourbon
- 1 sugar cube
- 2 dashes bitters
- Ice
- Orange peel

Instructions:

1. Muddle sugar and bitters in a glass.
2. Add bourbon and ice, stir well.
3. Garnish with orange peel.

Smoked Almonds

Ingredients:

- 200g almonds
- 1 tsp smoked paprika
- 1 tbsp olive oil
- ½ tsp salt

Instructions:

1. Toss almonds with oil, paprika, and salt.
2. Bake at 180°C for 10 minutes.

Mojito & Cuban Chicken Skewers

Mojito

Ingredients:

- 50ml white rum
- 1 tbsp sugar
- 8 mint leaves
- 25ml lime juice
- Soda water

Instructions:

1. Muddle mint and sugar with lime juice.
2. Add rum and ice, top with soda.

Cuban Chicken Skewers

Ingredients:

- 2 chicken breasts, cubed
- 1 tsp cumin
- 1 tsp lime juice
- 1 tbsp olive oil

Instructions:

1. Marinate chicken for 30 minutes.
2. Grill until golden.

Espresso Martini & Chocolate-Dipped Biscotti

Espresso Martini

Ingredients:

- 50ml vodka
- 25ml coffee liqueur
- 25ml espresso
- Ice

Instructions:

1. Shake all ingredients with ice and strain into a glass.

Chocolate-Dipped Biscotti

Ingredients:

- 100g biscotti
- 100g dark chocolate

Instructions:

1. Melt chocolate and dip biscotti halfway.
2. Let set before serving.

Manhattan & Mini Beef Sliders

Manhattan

Ingredients:

- 50ml rye whiskey
- 20ml sweet vermouth
- 2 dashes bitters
- Ice
- Cherry

Instructions:

1. Stir whiskey, vermouth, and bitters with ice.
2. Strain into a glass, garnish with a cherry.

Mini Beef Sliders

Ingredients:

- 200g ground beef
- 4 mini buns
- 1 tbsp mustard
- Cheese slices

Instructions:

1. Form beef into small patties and grill.
2. Assemble with mustard and cheese in buns.

French 75 & Goat Cheese Crostini

French 75

Ingredients:

- 30ml gin
- 15ml lemon juice
- 10ml sugar syrup
- Champagne

Instructions:

1. Shake gin, lemon juice, and sugar syrup.
2. Strain into a flute and top with champagne.

Goat Cheese Crostini

Ingredients:

- 1 baguette, sliced
- 100g goat cheese
- 1 tbsp honey

Instructions:

1. Toast bread, spread with cheese.
2. Drizzle with honey.

Moscow Mule & Honey Sriracha Wings

Moscow Mule

Ingredients:

- 50ml vodka
- 25ml lime juice
- Ginger beer

Instructions:

1. Fill a glass with ice, add vodka and lime juice.
2. Top with ginger beer.

Honey Sriracha Wings

Ingredients:

- 500g chicken wings
- 2 tbsp honey
- 1 tbsp Sriracha

Instructions:

1. Bake wings at 200°C for 25 minutes.
2. Toss with honey and Sriracha.

Daiquiri & Coconut Shrimp

Daiquiri

Ingredients:

- 50ml white rum
- 25ml lime juice
- 15ml simple syrup
- Ice

Instructions:

1. Shake all ingredients with ice and strain into a chilled glass.

Coconut Shrimp

Ingredients:

- 200g shrimp, peeled
- 50g flour
- 1 egg, beaten
- 100g shredded coconut
- 50g panko breadcrumbs
- Oil for frying

Instructions:

1. Coat shrimp in flour, dip in egg, then roll in coconut and panko.
2. Fry until golden brown.

Whiskey Sour & Candied Bacon

Whiskey Sour

Ingredients:

- 50ml bourbon
- 25ml lemon juice
- 15ml simple syrup
- Ice
- 1 egg white (optional)

Instructions:

1. Shake all ingredients (without ice) to emulsify.
2. Add ice, shake again, strain into a glass.

Candied Bacon

Ingredients:

- 6 bacon slices
- 2 tbsp brown sugar
- 1 tbsp maple syrup
- ½ tsp black pepper

Instructions:

1. Coat bacon with sugar, syrup, and pepper.
2. Bake at 180°C for 15-20 minutes.

Aperol Spritz & Caprese Skewers

Aperol Spritz

Ingredients:

- 60ml Aperol
- 90ml prosecco
- 30ml soda water
- Ice
- Orange slice

Instructions:

1. Pour Aperol, prosecco, and soda into a glass.
2. Stir and garnish with an orange slice.

Caprese Skewers

Ingredients:

- 10 cherry tomatoes
- 10 mini mozzarella balls
- 10 basil leaves
- 1 tbsp balsamic glaze

Instructions:

1. Skewer tomato, basil, and mozzarella.
2. Drizzle with balsamic glaze.

Paloma & Chili Lime Popcorn

Paloma

Ingredients:

- 50ml tequila
- 25ml grapefruit juice
- 10ml lime juice
- Soda water
- Ice

Instructions:

1. Mix tequila, grapefruit, and lime juice.
2. Add ice, top with soda water.

Chili Lime Popcorn

Ingredients:

- 100g popcorn
- ½ tsp chili powder
- ½ tsp lime zest
- 1 tbsp butter, melted

Instructions:

1. Toss popcorn with butter, chili powder, and lime zest.

Piña Colada & Grilled Pineapple Bites

Piña Colada

Ingredients:

- 50ml white rum
- 50ml coconut cream
- 100ml pineapple juice
- Ice

Instructions:

1. Blend all ingredients with ice.
2. Serve in a chilled glass.

Grilled Pineapple Bites

Ingredients:

- 1 pineapple, cubed
- 1 tbsp honey
- ½ tsp cinnamon

Instructions:

1. Toss pineapple with honey and cinnamon.
2. Grill until caramelized.

Sidecar & Brie-Stuffed Figs

Sidecar

Ingredients:

- 50ml cognac
- 25ml orange liqueur
- 25ml lemon juice
- Ice

Instructions:

1. Shake all ingredients with ice, strain into a glass.

Brie-Stuffed Figs

Ingredients:

- 6 figs, halved
- 50g Brie cheese
- 1 tbsp honey

Instructions:

1. Stuff figs with Brie, drizzle with honey.
2. Bake at 180°C for 5 minutes.

Bloody Mary & Mini Lobster Rolls

Bloody Mary

Ingredients:

- 50ml vodka
- 100ml tomato juice
- 10ml lemon juice
- Dash of Worcestershire sauce
- Dash of hot sauce
- Celery stick

Instructions:

1. Mix all ingredients with ice, serve in a glass.

Mini Lobster Rolls

Ingredients:

- 100g cooked lobster meat
- 2 tbsp mayo
- 1 tsp lemon juice
- 4 mini brioche buns

Instructions:

1. Mix lobster with mayo and lemon juice.
2. Serve in mini buns.

Cosmopolitan & Smoked Salmon Canapés

Cosmopolitan

Ingredients:

- 40ml vodka
- 20ml cranberry juice
- 10ml lime juice
- 10ml orange liqueur
- Ice

Instructions:

1. Shake all ingredients with ice, strain into a glass.

Smoked Salmon Canapés

Ingredients:

- 6 crackers
- 50g smoked salmon
- 50g cream cheese
- 1 tsp lemon zest

Instructions:

1. Spread cream cheese on crackers.
2. Top with smoked salmon and lemon zest.

Gin & Tonic & Cucumber Avocado Toast

Gin & Tonic

Ingredients:

- 50ml gin
- 100ml tonic water
- Ice
- Lime wedge

Instructions:

1. Pour gin over ice, top with tonic.

Cucumber Avocado Toast

Ingredients:

- 2 slices bread
- 1 avocado, mashed
- ½ cucumber, sliced
- 1 tsp lemon juice

Instructions:

1. Spread avocado on toasted bread.
2. Top with cucumber slices.

Rum Punch & Jamaican Jerk Chicken Bites

Rum Punch

Ingredients:

- 50ml dark rum
- 50ml pineapple juice
- 25ml orange juice
- 15ml lime juice
- 10ml grenadine
- Ice

Instructions:

1. Shake all ingredients with ice and strain into a glass.

Jamaican Jerk Chicken Bites

Ingredients:

- 200g chicken breast, cubed
- 1 tbsp jerk seasoning
- 1 tbsp olive oil

Instructions:

1. Toss chicken with seasoning and oil.
2. Cook in a pan until golden brown.

Sazerac & Cajun Spiced Pecans

Sazerac

Ingredients:

- 50ml rye whiskey
- 1 sugar cube
- 2 dashes Peychaud's bitters
- 10ml absinthe (for rinse)
- Lemon twist

Instructions:

1. Muddle sugar and bitters, add whiskey.
2. Rinse glass with absinthe, pour mixture in.

Cajun Spiced Pecans

Ingredients:

- 200g pecans
- 1 tbsp butter, melted
- ½ tsp cayenne pepper
- ½ tsp paprika

Instructions:

1. Toss pecans with butter and spices.
2. Bake at 180°C for 10 minutes.

Pisco Sour & Peruvian Ceviche Cups

Pisco Sour

Ingredients:

- 50ml Pisco
- 25ml lime juice
- 15ml simple syrup
- 1 egg white
- Ice

Instructions:

1. Shake all ingredients without ice.
2. Add ice, shake again, strain into a glass.

Peruvian Ceviche Cups

Ingredients:

- 200g white fish, cubed
- 50ml lime juice
- 1 tbsp red onion, finely chopped
- ½ tsp salt
- 1 tbsp coriander, chopped

Instructions:

1. Marinate fish in lime juice for 10 minutes.
2. Mix with onion, salt, and coriander.
3. Serve in small cups.

Amaretto Sour & Almond-Crusted Brie Bites

Amaretto Sour

Ingredients:

- 50ml Amaretto
- 25ml lemon juice
- 10ml simple syrup
- 1 egg white (optional)
- Ice

Instructions:

1. Shake all ingredients without ice.
2. Add ice, shake again, strain into a glass.

Almond-Crusted Brie Bites

Ingredients:

- 200g Brie cheese, cubed
- 50g crushed almonds
- 1 egg, beaten

Instructions:

1. Dip Brie in egg, then coat with almonds.
2. Bake at 180°C for 10 minutes.

Bellini & Peach Prosciutto Wraps

Bellini

Ingredients:

- 50ml peach purée
- 100ml prosecco

Instructions:

1. Pour peach purée into a glass.
2. Top with prosecco, stir gently.

Peach Prosciutto Wraps

Ingredients:

- 6 peach slices
- 6 prosciutto slices
- 1 tbsp honey

Instructions:

1. Wrap peach slices with prosciutto.
2. Drizzle with honey.

Caipirinha & Brazilian Cheese Puffs

Caipirinha

Ingredients:

- 50ml cachaça
- ½ lime, cut into wedges
- 2 tsp sugar
- Ice

Instructions:

1. Muddle lime and sugar.
2. Add ice and cachaça, stir.

Brazilian Cheese Puffs

Ingredients:

- 200g tapioca flour
- 100ml milk
- 50g Parmesan cheese, grated
- 1 egg

Instructions:

1. Mix all ingredients, pour into mini muffin tins.
2. Bake at 180°C for 15 minutes.

Hot Toddy & Maple Glazed Nuts

Hot Toddy

Ingredients:

- 50ml whiskey
- 150ml hot water
- 1 tbsp honey
- 1 cinnamon stick

Instructions:

1. Stir whiskey, honey, and hot water together.
2. Add cinnamon stick.

Maple Glazed Nuts

Ingredients:

- 200g mixed nuts
- 2 tbsp maple syrup
- ½ tsp cinnamon

Instructions:

1. Toss nuts with maple syrup and cinnamon.
2. Bake at 180°C for 10 minutes.

Kir Royale & Raspberry Dark Chocolate Tartlets

Kir Royale

Ingredients:

- 10ml crème de cassis
- 100ml champagne

Instructions:

1. Pour crème de cassis into a flute.
2. Top with champagne.

Raspberry Dark Chocolate Tartlets

Ingredients:

- 6 mini tart shells
- 100g dark chocolate, melted
- 12 raspberries

Instructions:

1. Fill tart shells with melted chocolate.
2. Top with raspberries.

Dark & Stormy & Spicy Ginger Meatballs

Dark & Stormy

Ingredients:

- 50ml dark rum
- 100ml ginger beer
- 10ml lime juice
- Ice

Instructions:

1. Fill glass with ice, pour in rum and lime juice.
2. Top with ginger beer.

Spicy Ginger Meatballs

Ingredients:

- 200g ground beef
- 1 tbsp ginger, grated
- ½ tsp chili flakes
- 1 tbsp soy sauce

Instructions:

1. Mix all ingredients, form into small meatballs.
2. Bake at 180°C for 15 minutes.

Mai Tai & Crispy Coconut Chicken Bites

Mai Tai

Ingredients:

- 30ml white rum
- 30ml dark rum
- 15ml orange liqueur
- 15ml lime juice
- 10ml orgeat syrup
- 5ml simple syrup
- Ice

Instructions:

1. Shake all ingredients with ice and strain into a glass.
2. Garnish with a lime wedge and mint sprig.

Crispy Coconut Chicken Bites

Ingredients:

- 200g chicken breast, cut into strips
- 50g shredded coconut
- 50g panko breadcrumbs
- 1 egg, beaten
- 50g flour
- ½ tsp salt

Instructions:

1. Dredge chicken in flour, then egg, then coconut-panko mix.
2. Fry until golden brown and crispy.

Tom Collins & Lemon Basil Bruschetta

Tom Collins

Ingredients:

- 50ml gin
- 25ml lemon juice
- 15ml simple syrup
- 100ml soda water
- Ice

Instructions:

1. Shake gin, lemon juice, and simple syrup with ice.
2. Strain into a glass, top with soda.

Lemon Basil Bruschetta

Ingredients:

- 6 slices of baguette
- 1 tbsp olive oil
- 1 tomato, diced
- ½ tsp lemon zest
- 4 basil leaves, chopped

Instructions:

1. Toast baguette slices.
2. Mix tomato, lemon zest, and basil; spoon onto bread.

Irish Coffee & Whiskey Caramel Truffles

Irish Coffee

Ingredients:

- 50ml Irish whiskey
- 100ml hot coffee
- 1 tbsp brown sugar
- 25ml heavy cream

Instructions:

1. Stir whiskey and sugar into hot coffee.
2. Gently float cream on top.

Whiskey Caramel Truffles

Ingredients:

- 100g dark chocolate, melted
- 50ml heavy cream
- 1 tbsp whiskey
- 1 tbsp caramel sauce
- Cocoa powder (for dusting)

Instructions:

1. Mix melted chocolate, cream, whiskey, and caramel.
2. Chill, roll into balls, dust with cocoa powder.

Blue Lagoon & Shrimp Ceviche Shots

Blue Lagoon

Ingredients:

- 50ml vodka
- 25ml blue curaçao
- 100ml lemonade
- Ice

Instructions:

1. Shake vodka and curaçao with ice.
2. Strain into a glass, top with lemonade.

Shrimp Ceviche Shots

Ingredients:

- 200g cooked shrimp, chopped
- 50ml lime juice
- 1 tbsp red onion, finely chopped
- 1 tbsp coriander, chopped
- ½ tsp salt

Instructions:

1. Marinate shrimp in lime juice for 10 minutes.
2. Mix with onion, coriander, and salt.
3. Serve in shot glasses.

Hurricane & New Orleans Beignets

Hurricane

Ingredients:

- 50ml dark rum
- 50ml passion fruit juice
- 25ml orange juice
- 10ml lime juice
- 10ml grenadine
- Ice

Instructions:

1. Shake all ingredients with ice.
2. Strain into a glass, garnish with an orange slice.

New Orleans Beignets

Ingredients:

- 250g flour
- 1 tsp baking powder
- 50g sugar
- 150ml milk
- 1 egg
- Oil for frying
- Powdered sugar (for dusting)

Instructions:

1. Mix flour, baking powder, sugar, milk, and egg into a dough.
2. Roll out, cut into squares, fry until golden.
3. Dust with powdered sugar.

Champagne Cocktail & Smoked Gouda Puffs

Champagne Cocktail

Ingredients:

- 1 sugar cube
- 2 dashes Angostura bitters
- 100ml champagne

Instructions:

1. Soak sugar cube in bitters.
2. Drop into a flute and top with champagne.

Smoked Gouda Puffs

Ingredients:

- 100ml water
- 50g butter
- 60g flour
- 2 eggs
- 50g smoked Gouda, grated

Instructions:

1. Boil water and butter, stir in flour.
2. Beat in eggs, add Gouda.
3. Pipe onto a tray, bake at 180°C for 20 minutes.

Mint Julep & Bourbon Glazed Wings

Mint Julep

Ingredients:

- 50ml bourbon
- 10 mint leaves
- 2 tsp sugar
- Crushed ice

Instructions:

1. Muddle mint and sugar.
2. Add bourbon, top with ice, stir.

Bourbon Glazed Wings

Ingredients:

- 500g chicken wings
- 50ml bourbon
- 2 tbsp honey
- 1 tbsp soy sauce
- ½ tsp chili flakes

Instructions:

1. Toss wings with bourbon, honey, soy sauce, and chili flakes.
2. Bake at 200°C for 25 minutes.

White Russian & Espresso Brownie Bites

White Russian

Ingredients:

- 50ml vodka
- 25ml coffee liqueur
- 25ml cream
- Ice

Instructions:

1. Pour vodka and coffee liqueur over ice.
2. Float cream on top.

Espresso Brownie Bites

Ingredients:

- 100g dark chocolate, melted
- 50g butter
- 50g sugar
- 1 egg
- 30ml espresso
- 50g flour

Instructions:

1. Mix all ingredients into a batter.
2. Pour into mini molds, bake at 180°C for 15 minutes.

Black Velvet & Oysters on the Half Shell

Black Velvet

Ingredients:

- 100ml stout beer
- 100ml champagne

Instructions:

1. Pour stout into a flute.
2. Gently top with champagne.

Oysters on the Half Shell

Ingredients:

- 6 fresh oysters
- 1 tbsp lemon juice
- 1 tsp shallots, minced
- ½ tsp black pepper

Instructions:

1. Shuck oysters, place on ice.
2. Drizzle with lemon juice, sprinkle with shallots and pepper.

Gimlet & Avocado Deviled Eggs

Gimlet

Ingredients:

- 50ml gin
- 25ml lime juice
- 15ml simple syrup
- Ice

Instructions:

1. Shake all ingredients with ice.
2. Strain into a chilled coupe glass.

Avocado Deviled Eggs

Ingredients:

- 6 hard-boiled eggs
- 1 ripe avocado
- 1 tbsp lime juice
- ½ tsp salt
- ½ tsp smoked paprika

Instructions:

1. Mash avocado with egg yolks, lime juice, and salt.
2. Pipe into egg whites, sprinkle with paprika.

Zombie Cocktail & Hawaiian BBQ Skewers

Zombie Cocktail

Ingredients:

- 25ml light rum
- 25ml dark rum
- 15ml apricot liqueur
- 15ml lime juice
- 50ml pineapple juice
- 5ml grenadine
- Ice

Instructions:

1. Shake all ingredients with ice.
2. Strain into a tiki glass and garnish with a pineapple slice.

Hawaiian BBQ Skewers

Ingredients:

- 300g chicken breast, cubed
- 1 tbsp soy sauce
- 1 tbsp pineapple juice
- ½ tsp ginger
- Pineapple chunks
- Bell pepper chunks

Instructions:

1. Marinate chicken in soy sauce, pineapple juice, and ginger.
2. Thread onto skewers with pineapple and peppers.
3. Grill until golden brown.

Brandy Alexander & Hazelnut Shortbread

Brandy Alexander

Ingredients:

- 40ml brandy
- 25ml crème de cacao
- 25ml heavy cream
- Ice

Instructions:

1. Shake all ingredients with ice.
2. Strain into a coupe glass and sprinkle with nutmeg.

Hazelnut Shortbread

Ingredients:

- 100g butter
- 50g sugar
- 150g flour
- 30g ground hazelnuts

Instructions:

1. Cream butter and sugar, mix in flour and hazelnuts.
2. Roll into dough, cut into shapes, bake at 180°C for 12 minutes.

Clover Club & Raspberry Macarons

Clover Club

Ingredients:

- 50ml gin
- 25ml lemon juice
- 15ml raspberry syrup
- 1 egg white
- Ice

Instructions:

1. Dry shake all ingredients, then shake again with ice.
2. Strain into a coupe glass.

Raspberry Macarons

Ingredients:

- 100g almond flour
- 100g powdered sugar
- 2 egg whites
- 50g granulated sugar
- 50g raspberry jam

Instructions:

1. Whip egg whites and granulated sugar into stiff peaks.
2. Fold in almond flour and powdered sugar.
3. Pipe onto a baking sheet, bake at 150°C for 15 minutes.
4. Sandwich with raspberry jam.

Aviation & Lavender Honey Toast Points

Aviation

Ingredients:

- 50ml gin
- 15ml maraschino liqueur
- 10ml crème de violette
- 15ml lemon juice
- Ice

Instructions:

1. Shake all ingredients with ice.
2. Strain into a coupe glass.

Lavender Honey Toast Points

Ingredients:

- 4 slices of baguette
- 1 tbsp honey
- ½ tsp dried lavender

Instructions:

1. Toast baguette slices.
2. Drizzle with honey and sprinkle with lavender.

Tequila Sunrise & Mango Habanero Salsa

Tequila Sunrise

Ingredients:

- 50ml tequila
- 100ml orange juice
- 10ml grenadine
- Ice

Instructions:

1. Pour tequila and orange juice over ice.
2. Slowly pour grenadine so it sinks.

Mango Habanero Salsa

Ingredients:

- 1 ripe mango, diced
- ½ habanero, finely chopped
- 1 tbsp lime juice
- ½ tsp salt

Instructions:

1. Mix all ingredients and let sit for 10 minutes.
2. Serve with tortilla chips.

Vesper Martini & Truffle Mushroom Arancini

Vesper Martini

Ingredients:

- 60ml gin
- 20ml vodka
- 10ml Lillet Blanc
- Ice

Instructions:

1. Shake all ingredients with ice.
2. Strain into a chilled martini glass.

Truffle Mushroom Arancini

Ingredients:

- 200g cooked risotto
- 50g mozzarella, cubed
- 30g Parmesan, grated
- 1 tsp truffle oil
- 50g breadcrumbs
- 1 egg, beaten

Instructions:

1. Mix risotto, Parmesan, and truffle oil.
2. Form into balls around a mozzarella cube.
3. Coat in egg and breadcrumbs, then fry until golden.

Planter's Punch & Jerk-Spiced Plantain Chips

Planter's Punch

Ingredients:

- 50ml dark rum
- 25ml lime juice
- 10ml grenadine
- 100ml pineapple juice
- Ice

Instructions:

1. Shake all ingredients with ice.
2. Strain into a tiki glass.

Jerk-Spiced Plantain Chips

Ingredients:

- 2 ripe plantains, thinly sliced
- 1 tbsp olive oil
- 1 tsp jerk seasoning

Instructions:

1. Toss plantain slices with oil and jerk seasoning.
2. Bake at 180°C for 15 minutes.

Spritz Veneziano & Olive Tapenade Crostini

Spritz Veneziano

Ingredients:

- 60ml Aperol
- 90ml prosecco
- 30ml soda water
- Ice

Instructions:

1. Pour Aperol over ice.
2. Add prosecco and soda water.

Olive Tapenade Crostini

Ingredients:

- 8 slices of baguette
- 50g black olives
- 1 garlic clove
- 1 tbsp olive oil

Instructions:

1. Blend olives, garlic, and olive oil into a paste.
2. Spread onto toasted baguette slices.

Mezcal Margarita & Grilled Elote Bites

Mezcal Margarita

Ingredients:

- 50ml mezcal
- 25ml lime juice
- 15ml agave syrup
- 10ml Cointreau
- Tajín seasoning (for rim)
- Ice

Instructions:

1. Rim glass with lime and dip in Tajín.
2. Shake mezcal, lime juice, agave, and Cointreau with ice.
3. Strain into a rocks glass over fresh ice.

Grilled Elote Bites

Ingredients:

- 2 ears corn, grilled and cut into rounds
- 2 tbsp mayonnaise
- 1 tbsp cotija cheese, crumbled
- ½ tsp chili powder
- 1 tbsp cilantro, chopped
- 1 lime, cut into wedges

Instructions:

1. Brush grilled corn rounds with mayo.
2. Sprinkle with cotija cheese, chili powder, and cilantro.
3. Serve with lime wedges.

Boulevardier & Gorgonzola-Stuffed Dates

Boulevardier

Ingredients:

- 40ml bourbon
- 25ml sweet vermouth
- 25ml Campari
- Ice

Instructions:

1. Stir all ingredients with ice.
2. Strain into a rocks glass over a large ice cube.

Gorgonzola-Stuffed Dates

Ingredients:

- 10 Medjool dates, pitted
- 50g gorgonzola cheese
- 10 pecan halves

Instructions:

1. Stuff each date with gorgonzola.
2. Top with a pecan half.

Hanky Panky & Spicy Chorizo Empanadas

Hanky Panky

Ingredients:

- 50ml gin
- 25ml sweet vermouth
- 5ml Fernet-Branca
- Ice

Instructions:

1. Stir all ingredients with ice.
2. Strain into a coupe glass.

Spicy Chorizo Empanadas

Ingredients:

- 200g chorizo, crumbled
- ½ onion, diced
- 1 tsp smoked paprika
- 1 package empanada dough
- 1 egg, beaten

Instructions:

1. Cook chorizo and onion until golden.
2. Spoon into empanada dough, fold and seal edges.
3. Brush with egg wash and bake at 190°C for 20 minutes.

Jungle Bird & Crispy Duck Spring Rolls

Jungle Bird

Ingredients:

- 45ml dark rum
- 20ml Campari
- 45ml pineapple juice
- 15ml lime juice
- 10ml simple syrup
- Ice

Instructions:

1. Shake all ingredients with ice.
2. Strain into a rocks glass over ice.

Crispy Duck Spring Rolls

Ingredients:

- 200g duck breast, shredded
- 2 tbsp hoisin sauce
- 1 spring onion, sliced
- 8 spring roll wrappers
- 1 egg, beaten

Instructions:

1. Mix duck with hoisin sauce and spring onion.
2. Roll into wrappers and seal with egg wash.
3. Fry until crispy and golden.

Bee's Knees & Honey Glazed Pistachios

Bee's Knees

Ingredients:

- 50ml gin
- 20ml lemon juice
- 15ml honey syrup
- Ice

Instructions:

1. Shake all ingredients with ice.
2. Strain into a coupe glass.

Honey Glazed Pistachios

Ingredients:

- 100g pistachios
- 2 tbsp honey
- ½ tsp sea salt

Instructions:

1. Warm honey in a pan, add pistachios and stir to coat.
2. Spread on parchment paper and sprinkle with salt.
3. Let cool before serving.

www.ingramcontent.com/pod-product-compliance
Lightning Source LLC
LaVergne TN
LVHW081333060526
838201LV00055B/2627